SPECULATIVE POETS OF TEXAS

Volume I

Edited by Dr. Malia A. Pérez

Other Books Available From
The House Of The Fighting Chupacabras Press

Live From La Pryor: The Poetry Of Juan Manuel Pérez, A Zavala County Native Son, Volume One
Edited by Dr. Malia A. Pérez with Juan Manuel Pérez

An Evaluative Case Study On The Efficacy Of The ELPS Program In Mathematics
By Dr. Malia A. Pérez

Sex, Lies, And Chupacabras
By Juan Manuel Pérez

A Poetry Anthology By C. E. C. Students Volume I: Spring 2014-Spring 2015
Edited by Juan Manuel Pérez and Dr. Malia A. Pérez

O' Dark Heaven: A Response To Suzette Haden Elgin's Definition Of Horror, 2nd Edition
By Juan Manuel Pérez

Speculative Poets Of Texas, Volume I
Edited by Dr. Malia A. Pérez

SPECULATIVE POETS OF TEXAS ®

THE HOUSE OF THE FIGHTING CHUPACABRAS PRESS

All rights reserved. No part of this book may be reproduced, stored in a retrieval system or transmitted in any form or by any means without the prior, written permission from the individual contributors and/or the publisher, except by a reviewer who may quote brief passages in a review to be printed in a newspaper, magazine, or journal.

Front/Back Cover Art by **Charles Ligocky**

All poetry is property of the individual poets and is only used here as part of this collection. All poetry rights return back to their respective authors and remain their sole property.

© 2015   Speculative Poets Of Texas, Volume I
           Edited by Dr. Malia A. Pérez

© 2015   The House Of The Fighting Chupacabras Press

          First printing

          ISBN: 978-1511905107

             www.hotfcpress.com

IN GOD WE TRUST

Table Of Contents

A Word From The Editor   11

PETER HOLLAND

A Ghost Story	17
La Lechusa Can Smile	18
A Robot's Christmas	19
At The Wake	20
Crone Song	21
Draugr	22
Explorer 4	24
La Calavera	25
La Lechusa	26
La Llorona	27
Man Beneath The Surface	28
Man's New Day	29
More And Less Human	30
No Tomorrow	31
Promises Broken	32
The Guardian	33
The Listening Post	34
The Old Woman	35
Voodoo Moon	36
You Say I Am Lost	37

JOE R. LANSDALE

So The Light Dims	43
Alone Among The Toothy Blooms	44
A Strange Poem	46
Moon In A Cistern	48
Friends	49
Little Words	50
Horrors Too True To Reveal	52
Soul On The Wall	53
When I Saw	54
Homesick In Rome	56
Between The Rising And The Setting Of The Sun	57
Bob	58
Waiting	61
Poetry Reading	62
Waking Up	64
When You're Mad	65
When I Came Down To Breakfast	66
I Saw Death In Town The Other Day	68
I Lie Awake	69
An Alien Poem	70

JUAN MANUEL PÉREZ

Comic Book Love Affair	78
A Sonnet For Rosie	80
Saint Batman	81
The Night Before Christmas At The Hall Of Justice	82
Secrets From The Batcave	85
El Chupacabra: An Introduction	86
Miff-ology	87
I Am Chupacabra	88
Ancient Wings	90
The Ballad Of The Brazen Ufologist	91
Opinionated	92
Walking Around The Compound On My Day Off	93
Interstellar Drunk	94
Pumpkins Despair	95
The Cemetery Caretaker	96
Vanity	98
Red Is The Barn	99
Waiting	100
Requiem For Satan	101
Full Moon Love	102

WAIDE AARON RIDDLE

Potions, Potions, Potions	110
The Court Jester	112
The Wedding Of The Dead	114
Blackraven	115
Something Wicked Dwells	116
Handsome	118
Dinner Tonight... With Friends	121
Ghost Tellers	122
Dark Circus	124
The Dance Of The Ghosts	126
A Haunting In Arkansas/The Evil Evening	127
31 October Street	128
The Halloween Lullaby	129
Auschwitz	130
Bayou's Hex	132
Jack O' Lantern Fever	135
Beautiful Blue	136
Beginner's Spell	137
Excerpt From The Poem: "The Chocolate Man: A Children's Horror Tale"	138
Black Night	142

RIE SHERIDAN ROSE

Sibling Rivalry	149
Chains Of Straw-Ropes Of Gold	155
Down In The Hollow	164
My Boyfriend's Dead	166
A Treatise On Spell Components	168
By Candlelight	169
Best Be Ware	170
Outdated	172
And The Skeletons Will Kick Your Ass	175
To Tell Medusa No…	176
Concerning The Burning Of Witches In Salem	178
Annabel Dawn	180
Raise A Glass In Parting	182
Ain't That The Way?	184
The Soul Of A Harper	186
Midnight Encounter	188
The Standing Stones	190
Ride The Red Wind	191
The Bridge Of Birds	192
The Starlight Bathing	195
About The Cover Artist: *CHARLES LIGOCKY*	197

A Word From The Editor

Texas is known for a lot of things, most of them big, wild, and with a country, barbeque flare and a touch of spicy, Mexican flavor. Among all that is majestic about this great state are its tremendous poets, spectacular with western vernacular or Latin professorship. But then there are those few still among them who talk about the strange, the bizarre, the dark underbelly of myth and lore or of faraway lands or distant times and futures' past in the skies over the former or later, Lone Star State. These Texas poets are those whose work does not always fit in or sit well among the ordinary things poets talk about in general. These bards are called Speculative Poets and these particular ones found within this anthology were either born in Texas or got here as quick as there imagination could get them. Writing abundant, speculative poetry and a strong Texas claim were the only two requirements to be included within.

Join us here today, right now, for our first set of five Speculative Poets Of Texas (S.P.O.T.) with this first, large volume of hopefully more poetry anthologies to come. Read on as each poet takes you to places you might never venture on your own or perhaps to a fantastic place you wished you lived in instead of wherever you are in the real world.

We, at The House Of The Fighting Chupacabras Press, hope you enjoy the heck out of these great, Speculative Poets Of Texas. We also hope you recommend this book to others as much as we have enjoyed gathering these poets together for your reading enjoyment.

Dr. Malia A. Pérez

Peter Holland

Peter Holland

Peter Holland is a life-long San Antonian. He holds a Bachelor Degree in History from the University Of Texas-San Antonio (UTSA). He is a member of the Alamo Area Poets Association. The beauty of the land and its history are an endless wellspring for his inspired pen. He shares his love of the place and of words at several local open mic events in and around the town he so loves. He had his chapbook, *A Year in South Texas*, published by Pecan Grove Press in 2009.

About His Poems:

A Ghost Story is appearing here for the first time anywhere.

La Lechusa Can Smile is appearing here for the first time anywhere.

A Robot's Christmas is appearing here for the first time anywhere.

At The Wake is appearing here for the first time anywhere.

Crone Song is appearing here for the first time anywhere.

Draugr is appearing here for the first time anywhere.

Explorer 4 is appearing here for the first time anywhere.

La Calavera is appearing here for the first time anywhere.

La Lechusa is appearing here for the first time anywhere.

La Llorona is appearing here for the first time anywhere.

Man Beneath The Surface is appearing here for the first time anywhere.

Man's New Day is appearing here for the first time anywhere.

More And Less Human is appearing here for the first time anywhere.

No Tomorrow is appearing here for the first time anywhere.

Promises Broken is appearing here for the first time anywhere.

The Guardian is appearing here for the first time anywhere.

The Listening Post is appearing here for the first time anywhere.

The Old Woman is appearing here for the first time anywhere.

Voodoo Moon is appearing here for the first time anywhere.

You Say I Am Lost is appearing here for the first time anywhere.

A Ghost Story

As I enter the forgotten room
the strains of an etude rise from
the long unused grand piano.
But looking, I find only a puddle
of silver light washing the keys.
As I stare the tune becomes
strident growing in volume,
becoming angry and violent.
The room, never warm, began
to grow cold as a winter night.
I have trespassed here.
I saw the first small object move,
a small stone of glass flew out,
from shadow though moonlight
to mare the paper by my head.
I fear I have offended our ghost.

La Lechusa Can Smile

Every other boy in town
looks away,
walks faster,
or walks on the other side of the path
when they pass the dark old jacal
the old woman lives in,
but not Pedro.
He walks right up to her gate
wraps on the gray cedar boards
calling out, "Tia Bruja!"
She comes out smiles on Pedro.
He asks how she is, if she needs
any little thing done, or repaired.
She gives him a candy and they part.
Pedro has good reason to love her.
She saved his mother from filling
a sad space in the Campo Santo,
Tia Bruja took the fever away.
Pedro knows what she is,
why should he care?
Owls are singing again.
It will be a good night for Pedro.

A Robot's Christmas

He had served many masters.
Now, he was to man the controls.
What an odd thing for a robot.
He was to pilot the master's ship
while the master was suspended.
Sleeping the cold sleep of space men.
From Jupiter to Earth was a long trip
the Paradise was too small a ship for
all the food and water required
for a man on such a great long trip.
The robot looked at the console,
"It is Christmas Day," it said to no one.
It processed a memory. Its last Christmas
on the moon of Io with the miners,
drunken song and gaiety, for as much
as it could miss a thing it did those days.
A light began to flash, a siren to sound.
A stone the size of a chestnut tore through
the ship, damaging many of the ships systems.
The Paradise began to spin madly,
bucking like a great wild beast.
Death was slow but violent for Paradise.
"Trouble in Paradise." the robot quipped
before its head crashed into a bulk head.
Before it powered off it said, to no one,
in a voice so very small, "God bless us every one."
The Paradise exploded.

At The Wake

Sure, the fiddles have all been put away,
the old folks sit in reverent silence
as we await dawn's rosy morning glow.
Fair old Mother Moon slips her cloudy cloak.
She spills her silvery light on dear old Mike.
He had fallen from the maple tree,
snapped his neck like a willowy reed.
In the morning Father Murphy would
put him in his soft and loamy bed,
but now he rests in polished pine.
What is this? His hollow eyes are open,
he is rising, sitting up, looking round.
Molly has fainted dead away on the floor.
The Magwires turn pale as fresh milk.
Misses Mike screams and passes out.
Mike tumbles out of his wooden box.
He stands kind of loose on his long legs.
His head is swimming from side to side.
Mike grabs hold of the lifeless Misses Mike.
He lets a hollow groan escape his curled lips.
As he lifts his wife to his jagged teeth
I swing the end iron at his once noble head,
crushing in his zombie skull with a sick thud.

Crone Song

The old crone sitting
beside the rickety bridge
stares into the stream.

What does the water show her?
Why man needs to fear water.

The old crone stands there
waiting for her next victim,
smiling inside.

What does she know is coming?
Why man needs to fear water.

The man comes along
going from mistress to wife,
leaving tears behind.

You fool something is coming.
You will learn to fear water.

Her laugh, a cackle,
gives the world something to fear
She flies before him.

The crone is what was coming.
He falls into the water.

Draugr

Mothers fright their children
with ghoulish things of the dark,
but in the wood of Arama Da
there is a thing of fetid flesh
with iced sea water for blood.
On the Irish coast in a season
all golden and warm, a man
from the far off north came,
raiding or trading it matters not.
He came upon a swine herd.
He demanded from him a pig.
The boy took up his cudgel
The north man laughed at him.
The north man moved his ax
to his thick sinewy hand.
Sprightly the boy evaded the blow
he struck with savage fury.
The north man lay as still as stone.
The boy rolled the dead man
into a pile stone out of the way
where worms went to their work.
The next full moon rose watery
it was an ill orb above all.
Out of the stones rose a draugr
A wretched fiend out of darkness
it mindlessly killed whatever
hapless thing crossed its path.

He is Death's firstborn son,
a fiend of neither heaven nor hell.
He wanders the wood a-killing
for the love of blood and death.

Explorer 4

The cold of Space was outside,
but the inside was just as cold.
The crew of Explorer 4,
Captain Lynn Mac and
Specialist Lopov, slept
safe in their sleep chambers.
All systems seemed "Go."
All the right lights flashed.
All the right chimes sung.
Now after months in space
they reached the end of their road.
They orbited red Mars.
When something went boom!
The computer seemed
to want to say, "Oh, no!"

La Calavera

Tall and elegant, she enters.
Every eye turns to her instantly.
Grace personified in black lace
as she steps upon the dance floor.
The young men jostle and vie
for her attention and her hand.
Oh, the one she comes to choose.
He is the worst of the young men
haughty, proud and most rough
in both speech and behavior.
The two dance all the night.
She makes him a fine dancer,
he demonstrates a deftness
we never saw in him before.
As the musicians prepare to leave,
the young men ask their ladies
for a token of the night and a kiss.
Our confident one does the same.
She nods lowering her lace veil.
There is but a grinning skull
staring vacantly back at him.

La Lechusa

You sit on your bridge
your clear eyes shining bright.
Your sad hoots are heard,
a dirge for mortal man,
coming into your sight.
Your talons rend flesh
of the foolish who cross
your black bridge above the fish.
You are the boss of the river.
Whether you are myth or
monster of darkest nightmare
man must heed your cries.

La Llorona

Have you heard the call of *La Llorona*?
¡Mijos! ¡Mijos!

She put her babies in the water.
Out of spite she put them in.
But she followed right behind.
¡Mijos! ¡Mijos!

Was he the devil *Mária*?
Your fancy man in black.
*Pápa t*o your little babies.
¡Mijos! ¡Mijos!

Could he have been a son of the Devil?
Was it *El Diablo* who led you here?
Led you to stand on this muddy bank?
¡Mijos! ¡Mijos!

Singing on this riverbank?
Singing for your babies?
Singing out *¡Mijos! ¡Mijos!*

Man Beneath The Surface

I am floating in a morass of cybernetics
I was placed here to be the soul
deep inside the machine,
made the consciousness of weapon.
Tomorrow's weapon wishes
they would have left me alone.
So little of me is left, getting lost is easy.
Memory holds me to the soul they desire.
Often, I wonder if my soul vanished
what would they do with what is left.

Man's New Day

For fifty years man planned, plotted, and schemed,
now, the first of the colony ships nestle
on the dust of the Bradbury Plains.
Alpha colony, the first of many,
will see things run smoothly.
Over the next weeks will land the many
infrastructure modules to house the workers
of the many jobs needed to keep man alive
where man is not native but desires to be.
But, for now news back on Mother Earth
is clamoring with the stories of success.
Man is no longer just an earthling.

More And Less Human

They gave me an option when it all began,
"Have the surgery or you will be dead."
So spine replaced along with hips, legs, and arms.
Skull removed with both ears and eyes.
Guts removed, replaced with nutrition pump
waste dealt with, filters take it away.
Soft body and brain covered in kevsteel,
even armor piercing round bounce off.
I am ten times the man I was, and less.
I am treated like the machine, not the man.
I still have feelings, desires, needs.
Even though my ability to meet them is gone.
I miss chit chat and small talk, even gossip.
They better remember their machine
has a man's soul locked inside.

No Tomorrow

When it all began it was adventure,
now, alone, staring into the abyss
between our solar system and the next,
I wonder how I was talked into this.
I sit in the only manned observatory
on the razor's edge of being lost
like a grain of sand in the ocean.
In ten years I have observed nothing.
Now, my systems fail randomly.
One day I will find I am bobbing lost,
looked for by an indifferent
and unsympathetic world.

Promises Broken

For a decade man toiled under the pink skies
building the hope of man in the red dust,
but one day back on Earth men gathered
to decide the fate of their fellows far away.
Once again the global economy tanked
leaving little for everyday running of things.
Luxury was to be cut away and burned off.
Mars became a luxury Earth could no longer afford.
A message was sent from Earth informing Mars,
Mother was abandoning her child in space.
They were to be cut off, isolated, left for dead.
After days of hand ringing the men of Mars
began to see the opportunity presented them.
Now no longer Earth men on Mars but Martians;
a people with a future promising and bright.

The Guardian

He stalks ancient avenues,
dusty streets of antiquity,
but history is the last thing
on his mind this moonless night.
His target is hiding ahead.
It's his job to eliminate
the threat and do it silently,
because he is behind the line,
deep in the enemies country.
But it's his job, his duty to keep
the nation safe from terror
and those who cause the terror.

The Listening Post

In my metal home on a rock
floating along with other rocks,
I listen to rebel communication.
For twenty-four months I have
been at this my lonely outpost.
I cannot speak to a living soul.
I am too far away for live chat.
I correspond with my office
in intercepted packets of data.
I have nine-hundred square feet.
I am beginning to believe
I am over run by gremlins.
Vital systems suddenly fail
and unfail just as suddenly.
I am hearing voices in the night,
but it is always night here.
I was told my relief would arrive
in twenty-four months. Can I last?
I just found out about the men
who held this post before me.
Three were suicides, two are rebels.
Two years ago I wondered why.
I think I understand them now.

The Old Woman

They say she is a widow,
but she has been old
such a very long time.
My Mommy still calls her
the mean old lady.
She is short, bent, frail.
She shuffles along,
withered hands holding
her old broomstick.
She wears only black
from her head to the ground.
A lacy black mantle
covers her dark silver hair.
Her milky eyes are dark,
but she knows her world.
The brave or foolish call her
Bruja, but not to her face.
You can find her sitting
on her little chair outside
her house beside the bridge.
But when the moon is full
we hear an owl wailing
high up in the trees;
then we know she's out
flying, searching for
the wicked, whoever it is.
Beware! *Lechuza* is flying.

Voodoo Moon

The old yellow moon's
reflection fills the still pool
hanging high above old cypress.
A beautiful black woman steps
from the inky bayou night.
She gets into her pirogue
sending shattering ripples out
distorting the face of the moon.
In the midst of the pool she sings
a sweet slow song of childhood
at the end she breaks an egg
letting its contents blend with
the still waters of the bayou.
From every direction of the night
a clamorous sound fills the dark.
Then, in their ones and twos
her minions come to her call.
Hollow-eyed with ragged limbs
they shamble out of the darkness.
Again she sings to them,
a song bitter and sweet to hear.
Her unwilling servants disappear
back into a Louisiana night
as she sits under her moon smiling.

You Say I Am Lost

He rose from his sleeping couch.
He half-floated down the corridor.
He passed both rec room and galley,
down and in toward the hub
on to the bridge of the craft.
The air was stale, scentless, and cold,
Grieg echoed in the solitude.
He sat in the chair of command.
The kind gentle voice of the computer
spoke in slow, even, emotionless tone,
"A problem has been detected.
We do not know where we are going."
The Navcom had failed to reboot
after the last maintenance power down.
He asked if it had detected chatter.
"Not for two full days." it replied.
"So we are lost?" "Yes."
"Tell me computer, how much food do I have?"
"At current rates, twenty-five years."
"And water?" "Indefinite." it said.
"So it was good I killed the crew, right?"
He made his way back to his sleeping couch.

Joe R. Lansdale

"Champion Mojo Storyteller

Joe R. Lansdale is the author
of over thirty novels and numerous short stories. His work has appeared in national anthologies, magazines, and collections, as well as numerous foreign publications. He has written for comics, television, film, newspapers, and Internet sites. His work has been collected in eighteen short-story collections, and he has edited or co-edited over a dozen anthologies. He has received the Edgar Award, eight Bram Stoker Awards, the Horror Writers Association Lifetime Achievement Award, the British Fantasy Award, the Grinzani Cavour Prize for Literature, the Herodotus Historical Fiction Award, the Inkpot Award for Contributions to Science Fiction and Fantasy, and many others. His novella Bubba Hotep was adapted to film by Don Coscarelli, starring Bruce Campbell and Ossie Davis. His story "Incident On and Off a Mountain Road" was adapted to film for Showtime's "Masters of Horror." He is currently co-producing several films, among them The Bottoms, based on his Edgar Award-winning novel, with Bill Paxton and Brad Wyman, and The Drive-In, with Greg Nicotero. He is Writer In Residence at Stephen F. Austin State University, and is the founder of the martial arts system Shen Chuan: Martial Science and its affiliate, Shen Chuan Family System. He is a member of both the United States and International Martial Arts Halls of Fame. He lives in Nacogdoches, Texas with his wife, dog, and two cats."

Biography is straight from his website:
http://joerlansdale.com/bio.html

About His Poems:

So The Light Dims previously appeared in the December 2013 issue of *TheHorrorZine.com.*

Alone Among The Toothy Blooms previously appeared in the May 2014 issue of *TheHorrorZine.com.*

A Strange Poem previously appeared in the December 2013 issue of *TheHorrorZine.com.*

Moon In A Cistern previously appeared in in the December 2013 issue of *TheHorrorZine.com.*

Friends previously appeared in the October 2013 issue of *TheHorrorZine.com.*

Little Words previously appeared in the December 2013 issue of *TheHorrorZine.com.*

Horrors Too True To Reveal previously appeared in the October 2013 issue of *TheHorrorZine.com.*

Soul On The Wall previously appeared in the October 2013 issue of *TheHorrorZine.com.*

When I Saw previously appeared in the July 2013 issue of *TheHorrorZine.com.*

Homesick In Rome previously appeared in the October 2013 issue of *TheHorrorZine.com.*

Between The Rising And The Setting Of The Sun previously appeared in the July 2013 issue of *TheHorrorZine.com.*

Bob previously appeared in the May 2013 issue of *TheHorrorZine.com.*

Waiting previously appeared in the May 2013 issue of *TheHorrorZine.com.*

Poetry Reading previously appeared in the May 2013 issue of *TheHorrorZine.com.*

Waking Up previously appeared in the May 2013 issue of *TheHorrorZine.com.*

When You're Mad previously appeared in the August 2012 issue of *TheHorrorZine.com.*

When I Came Down To Breakfast previously appeared in the October 2011 issue of *TheHorrorZine.com.*

I Saw Death In Town The Other Day previously appeared in the August 2012 issue of *TheHorrorZine.com.*

I Lie Awake previously appeared in the October 2011 issue of *TheHorrorZine.com.*

An Alien Poem previously appeared in the October 2011 issue of *TheHorrorZine.com.*

So The Light Dims

So the light dims
though the sun is out
and children play nearby
and a dog barks
and someone laughs
but the light fades
in my dark room
and I am embraced
in its shadowy arms
and I greet it with anticipation
for I am tired of life's
disappointments,
the sad expectations of a better world
that never comes
but taunts us with possibilities
like a dog howling at the moon
thinking it close sweet meat
not a spoiled boiled egg
full of false promise
so far away
So embrace me dark shadows
and lift me up on black wings
and carry me away
fast

Alone Among The Toothy Blooms

It's all right how things are now.
I feel no more alone than before it all.
More cautious perhaps,
but no more alone.
I handle myself well,
and some nights I mean that literally.
But what's a girl to do
at the end of the world,
when carnivorous flowers
bloom from skulls,
and vines move like the deep-sea tentacles of
squids and octopi
I hear voices sometimes,
in the distance,
but I dare not call out to them, for the blooms can
imitate a human voice,
and it must be them.
For who in their right mind
wanders down the street in the middle of the night crying out—
Good day. Good day. Have a nice day.
Though sometimes it fits when they mock words of an earlier
time when currency mattered.
Give me your money, asshole, and now.
Ah, there they go along the street, moonlight wet gold on their
blooms,
showing teeth inside of petals.
A dog barks.
Then whimpers.

Someone small screams.
I step back into the shadows.

A Strange Poem

Outside on the street,
I saw a strange poem
wearing nice shoes,
and pleated slacks.
Socks with dots,
baggy pants,
no hat.

We waved at each other.
I had arms.
It had words.
One of its words fell
into the storm drain
and splashed.

I laughed.
The poem chased me,
all the way home.
Its outside my window,
staring,
trying to get in.

I locked the doors.
I pulled the shades.
I went to the word processor
and wrote this down.
I looked outside my window.
The poem is gone.

Next morning,
outside,
I found its bloody tracks,
in the new
fallen
snow.

Moon In A Cistern

Face of a clown
down there and
rising,
red-nosed
and bloated
and drowned
Honk a horn
juggle some bones
he's a circus murder
killed by a monkey
with a juggling pin
One joke told too many
about bananas
and a cork in a big pig's ass
Sad in his over-sized shoes
rising from darkness
wet as an eel
clown car waiting
beside the cement well,
waiting to take him
in with the other
clowns,
tight together
as bright sardines
The monkey driving them
all straight
to
hell

Friends

I have my friends
I keep them close
propped up with
duct tape,
bound and gagged
in kitchen chairs
some are ill
some or weak
I think I forgot to feed them
And they care not at all
for the nails in their feet

Little Words

struggling over words
that know more holds
and have more tricks
that i do

they will not talk to me
even though i beg
quite nicely
instead they hide

i seek
they move
always just out of
reach

i wish i had
a butterfly net
within which
i could catch one

way i feel now
the word if caught
would take a bad bad
beating

please words
do not make me talk that way
deep down
you love me

kiss kiss
pet pet
i love you words
no need for a net

still they flee
fast
and easy over the paper
unwilling to stick

i go to bed
lonely
without my little
words

Horrors Too True To Reveal

There are some horrors
hard to discuss
dooms so dire you taste them
Terrors so sublime the skin crawls
But nothing quite matches
one particular grim view
that keeps us upstairs even though
our stomachs growl
and that would be grandma
and her hot blue
stretch pants at breakfast.

Soul On The Wall

Soul on the wall
Like shadows that crawl
Don't open the window
It's sure to fall
Soul on the wall
Like mice in the wall
Spiral down darkly
Lonely and bleak
Like blood on the sheets
Like flies in the meat
A dying bird call
Bats on the ceiling
Snakes in the sink
Bottles with skulls
Not fit to drink
Rock in the water
Parting the stream
Soul on the wall
Shadows that fall
Hungry rabid mice
at the edges of
damp skull walls

When I Saw

When I saw what had been done,
the bloody tub,
the knife and gun,
hair ripped out,
from my own head,
a knife cut across my wrist,
a .45 caliber bullet in my head,
slowly dying,
but still I could think,
I wish I had only bothered,
to write a note to make
you sad,
written it in lipstick
on the mirror above the sink,
because now I considered,
my death could make you glad,
and in a week,
a month,
a new girl will be in your bed,
she'll stain my sheets,
shit in our commode,
shave her legs in the tub,
wonder what the little
red spots are on the wall,
thinking them nail polish
from bubble bath moments,
while I painted my toes,
because I doubt you'll

tell her,
I killed myself,
my wrist bled out,
my brain leaked from a bullet hole,
and I died without
.....a....note.

Homesick In Rome

I wanted to write a poem
But I was in Rome
I don't write poetry in Rome
Only at home
There I have the pen I need
made of an old witch's finger,
the nail way long
And ink from the blood
of a freshly decapitated skull
The pen dipped
while the open eyes still see
and the mouth tries to work
And nearby I have nacho chips
And ice tea
And when I'm called to dinner
the kitchen is close
and the fresh corpse that went with
the head
is ready to eat
Then there's ice cream
Hopefully without any kind
of nuts in it
as I like it plain
and in a bowl
made from the top, sawed portion
of a skull
Afterward, maybe a musical on TV,
if it's a perfect kind of day.

Between The Rising And The Setting Of The Sun

The sun rises
The moon sets
And their beauty
Is divine
And in between
Those risings and settings
I think of how
To kill you
And get away with it
Without leaving DNA
But so far
The plan lies dormant
And I'm thinking it might
Best be done
At sea

Bob

We had a family friend named Bob.
We all liked Bob.
He had a nice house,
a nice car,
a boat.
He took us on boat trips,
me and my parents,
my baby sister.

Bob was all right.
He dressed a little odd,
wore a funny hat,
and his pants were too short,
his socks white,
his cheap leather shoes
shone bright as sunlight.

Bob moved away.
We missed him.
Some of the fun
went right out of
the neighborhood,
like air out of a balloon.

We felt uncomfortable,
however,
when two years after he
moved,
someone else bought
his property,
and tore down the house.

They found the bodies
of women in his basement,
one of them a teacher,
who was said to have run off.
But she didn't.

There were three others,
unidentified,
so far,
and as for Bob,
that wasn't his name,
or so the police said,
and they are still looking
for him.

Before he moved,
he gave us his boat.
I think about that.
Because under one
of the bench seats,
I found a woman's
sun hat,
with a spot on it,
bright red.

Maybe it's not blood,
but strawberry jam,
or paint,
but I stopped wearing it.

Waiting

Moving into this house,
being here for the first time,
and it still having goods
in the shelves,
and food in the refrigerator,
all of it spoiled,
I was most attracted to
the axe,
and that's why I invited
you over,
telling you the rental
was dirty,
and that I would appreciate
the kindness,
of help with the cleaning,
but actually,
when you get here,
thinking on how you
once left me
for another man,
something I can't forget,
no matter how much I smile,
I will be waiting,
behind the door,
with the axe.

Poetry Reading

Life is short and sweet
and how I love it,
bright with light,
and warm as an
oven,
I love it each day,
and I can't wait,
to see how it turns
out,
from year to year,
from date to date,
and then I go to a poetry
reading,
and I have to admit,
life seems less short
than I thought before,
it drones on and on,
and I'm nowhere near
a door.
Sadly,
I think of murder,
of all the poets,
especially the one with
a poem about a goddamn tree,
how it's beauty
is a part of her and me,
but that would be criminal,
so I just wait,

and wish for death,
hers or mine,
whichever will end this reading,
that goes on and on,
for endless time.

Waking Up

So I wake up
feeling like things
are all right,
and that I have a second
chance on life,
that I can make things
better than before,
and then I remember,
nope,
that's not likely,
because it wasn't a dream,
your body is still under the bed,
and my sheets,
and my hands,
are covered in blood.

When You're Mad

Don't try to run over anyone,
even if you really want to kill them,
because if you miss,
you might hit an armadillo,
or a sign,
or a big tree,
and you might kill yourself,
and the one you meant to hit,
will think you swerved to miss.

When I Came Down To Breakfast

When I came down to breakfast,
a large rhinoceros,
wearing Dad's bathrobe
was sitting in his chair,
a cup of coffee in front of him,
some toast on a plate,
partly eaten,
the newspaper in his hands,
glasses on his nose.
I could see what was left of Dad,
squashed beneath him,
flat,
between rhino ass and chair.
But the rhino was pleasant,
and asked if I needed eggs,
scrambled,
and I said yes,
and he got up to make them.
I saw then,
Dad,
Pancaked in the chair,
except where his arms and legs hung out.
Those were not smashed,
but the truth is,
I didn't care
one way or the other.

The eggs were good,
my lunch was packed,
and the rhino
gave me a pat on the back,
as I went out the door.

I Saw Death In Town The Other Day

I saw death in town the other day,
dressed up just like me.
I studied him real close.
A shadow of my former self
looked right back at me.

I do not think he's come just yet,
but he wanted me to know,
there will come a time,
not so far away,
when I will have to go.

He fretted over my thinning hair,
and ran my fingers through its strands
dragging them along,
like metal tines
through slender strips of sand.

When I walked away,
so did he,
leaving the store glass dark,
without image of either him,
or me
to look each other back
and see
the dead man that was to be.

I Lie Awake

I lie awake,
because everyone is dead,
and there is nothing better to do,
but listen to them,
outside,
those dead ones,
walking,
tapping on windows
and doors,
calling to me
in their dry voices,
to come outside,
and play,
but one look out there
shows me,
they have no toys.

An Alien Poem

You may think this is just a poem.
You'd be wrong.
It's a form of alien mind control.
We are the aliens.
This is our poem.
We write them because if you read them--
we got you.
You are now one of us.
We are taking over the world.
Problem.
It would take centuries
for enough people
to read poems
and become one of us.
Even poets don't read poetry.
Hell, can you blame them?
So, we're thinking of switching,
to encoding our thoughts
in pornographic websites
instead of poems,
or into car commercials.
We would get more people to become aliens
that way.
Whatever we decide to do
in the future,
this is the end of this poem,
and—
--HA!

We still got you sucker.
You should have stuck to video games.

Juan Manuel Pérez

Juan Manuel Pérez,

born and raised in the onion fields around La Pryor, Texas, is the author of four, full poetry collections, plus numerous poetry chapbooks and poetry workshop workbooks. The award-wining poet is also the 2011-2012 Poet Laureate for the San Antonio Poets Association, the Chupacabra Poet Laureate (lifetime), the 2014 Un-Official Hooters Poet, and the winner of the 2005 People's Comic Book Newsletter Award For Best Comic Book Poetry, as well as, the 31st Annual Southwest Texas Junior College Creative Arts Contest Over-All Literary Award Winner (Poetry & Prose) in 2012.

Currently, the author teaches, writes poetry, and chases chupacabras by the Texas Gulf Coast in Corpus Christi, Texas.

About His Poems:

Comic Book Love Affair previously appeared in *Deshogate: Amor Y Pazion*, Volume 1, Number 2, 2010, the Spring 2006 issue of *Comic Book Poetry Quarterly*, Volume 1, Number 2, and the January 2006 issue of the *Defender Of The Comic Book Faith*, Volume 1, Number 1.

A Sonnet For Rosie previously appeared in the Spring 2012 issue of *Harbinger Asylum.*

Saint Batman previously appeared in the March 2012 issue of *The Peoples Comic Book Newsletter*, Volume 16, Issue 134, and the Fall 2006 issue of *Comic Book Poetry Quarterly*, Volume 1, Number 4.

The Night Before Christmas At The Hall Of Justice previously appeared in the March 2009 issue of *The Peoples Comic Book Newsletter*, Volume 12, Issue 114.

Secrets From The Batcave previously appeared in the February 2012 issue of *TheHorrorZine.com.*

El Chupacabra: An Introduction previously appeared in a June 2012 Sunday Edition of the *San Antonio Express-News*.

Miff-ology previously appeared in July-September 2012 issue of *Star*Line: The Journal Of The Science Fiction Poetry Association*, Volume 35.3.

I Am Chupacabra previously appeared in *Boundless: The Anthology Of The Rio Grande Valley International Poetry Festival*, 2012.

Ancient Wings previously appeared in the *Langdon Review Of The Arts In Texas*, Volume 8, 2011-2012.

The Ballad Of The Brazen Ufologist previously appeared in the Fall 2012 issue of *Harbinger Asylum.*

Opinionated previously appeared in April-June 2011 issue of *Star*Line: The Journal Of The Science Fiction Poetry Association*, Volume 34.2.

Walking Around The Compound On My Day Off previously appeared in *The Eighth Continent: An Anthology Of Space Poems,* 2012.

Interstellar Drunk previously appeared in the 2011 *Mayo Review*, Texas A&M Commerce.

Pumpkins Despair previously appeared in *Inkwell Echoes: The 2011 Anthology Of The San Antonio Poets Association.*

The Cemetery Caretaker previously appeared in *Fresh Blood, Old Bones* by Biting Dog Press, 2012.

Vanity previously appeared in *Dwarf Stars 2012: The Best Speculative Short Poems Published in 2011,"* The 2012 Rhysling Anthology of the Best SF, Fantasy, And Horror

Poetry of 2011," and the March 2011 issue of ***Star*Line: The Journal Of The Science Fiction Poetry Association***, Volume 34.1.

Red Is The Barn previously appeared in the February 2011 issue of ***TheHorrorZine.com.***

Waiting is appearing here for the first time anywhere.

Requiem For Satan is appearing here for the first time anywhere.

Full Moon Love previously appeared in the March 2012 issue of ***Dark River Press.com.***

Comic Book Love Affair

To my 1980's comic book-hating, pyromaniac mother

Thunder and lightning
Paranoia across the sky
I shall pay dearly
This nasty habit won't die

Momma use to say,
"It's all wrong!"
So, she burned them all
That which to me belonged

She use to say
I was obsessed
Good Christian woman
Thought I was possessed

Tears of anger
For what I love
Dear mother
What were you thinking of?

Now I am grown
I have learned to forgive
But I am also married
Will history be relived?

I love her a lot…
But I love them too
They call to me
O, my mind is a zoo

This comic book love affair
Consumes most of me
O, this faithful sin of mine
It just won't let me be

I hope she understands
I hope they all understand
Never, ever, come between
A comic book and her man

A Sonnet For Rosie

The Jetson's Maid

Are your parts made in Japan
Your right leg, your left hand
Are you wired thru and thru
Head to toe, all of you

Are you able to feel my touch
Can you fake it or not so much
Do you know how to love
Not just roses and white doves

Are you able to fall asleep
Hope to wake and angels keep
Are you capable of dreaming
Is it syndicated or live and streaming

So can you be as much for me
As all the parts that make you be

Saint Batman

Inspired by the work of David Perry and Valentine Popov

Judge, jury, and executioner
Dark vigilante disposing human rights
The New American Jesus Christ
Against injustice he leads the fight

Too many questions for unwanted answers
Bare the creature of our common plight
Defeating our fears with guns and fists
Beautiful, yet corrupt, all in one sight

The controversial cure that everyone needs
Yet no one dares the claim
The dawn of Saint Batman
Through the darkness of the same

Hate him, because he wants to save you
Love him, because you know he will

The Night Before Christmas At The Hall Of Justice

A modern retelling of Clement Clarke Moore's
'Twas The Night Before Christmas (1822)

It was the night before Christmas and all through the Hall,
Not a villain was stirring. No not at all.
The colorful tights were all hung by the doorway with care,
In hopes that Super Santa soon will be there.
The Super Friends were all nestled all snug in their bed,
While visions of crime fighting danced in their heads.
Wonder Woman with lasso, Batman in his cowl,
Had just settled down from a long evening's prowl.
When outside the Hall, there arose such a clatter,
Superman sprung up from his slumber to see what's the matter.
Up and away to the window like Flash,
Busted open the blinds, almost broke all the glass.
As Metropolis' lights shinned on the falling fresh snow,
That gave clear as day sight to all things there below.
When to Kal-El's wondering eyes should appear,
But a small craft with eight funny looking reindeer.
And a short looking driver, so quirky and slick,
It took a few seconds to guess it's Super Saint Nick.
Slightly quicker than villains his coursers they came,
As he grunted and shouted and called each by name.
Now Clayface! Now Joker! Now Two Face and Black Manta!
On Riddler! On Bizarro! On Braniac and Giganta!
From the frozen reflection pool to the top of the wall,
Now quick away! Fly away! Fast away all!

As balloons that before the wild Joker let fly,
When they gather as one as they rise to the sky.
So up the Hall of Justice the coursers they flew,
With a flying craft of stuff and Super Santa too.
With fantastic hearing, he heard on the roof,
The bustling and shuffling of each of their hoof.
As Kal-El focused inward and was turning around,
Down came Super Santa in with a bound.
He was dressed mostly in purple from his head to his foot,
And his digs were all tarnished with lots of ashes and soot.
Orange bags he carried upon his small little back,
Looking more like a criminal about to fill his sack.
The Trouble Alert had not sounded upon this seasonal intrusion,
As the son of Krypton watched it all
     contemplating his confusion.
Reminiscing of an imp from within the 5th Dimension,
Purple derby, purple suit, going bald not to mention.
A half-smoked Cuban cigar he had tightly within his teeth,
As the smell permeated the room making it hard to breathe.
His face slightly round with cheeks that jiggled like jelly,
And a nice green bowtie about a foot up from his belly.
He was short, yet plump, like a happy little elf.
Superman laughed away at the sight, still unsure of himself.
Within a blink of his eye and a turn of his head,
Soon made Kal-El feel nothing to dread.
Super Santa bothered none and went straight to work,
Filled up all the tights then turned with a jerk.
Snapping his fingers like someone who definitely knows,
A single leap up the rooftop, quickly he rose.
He fled to his craft, his team he prepared,
Like the Bat Plane he flew, directly to air.

Superman heard him declare as he flew away from the hall:
Merry Christmas Super Friends! Merry Christmas to all!

Secrets From The Batcave

Attempting to hide that dark of me
Under this castle all can see
Hero, for those that justice seek
Villain, the rest who all is bleak

If truth be told, you'd understand
That justice needs its evil hand
That death and dying should ensue
What then your laws upon review

How then did they confess the deed
Without misdeed returned indeed
The secret shared, now look away
So coy the victory that rules the day

As evil doers endure their rite
In acts that hide the truth from site
Favors the plan remain in play
For truth, justice, the American way

El Chupacabra: An Introduction

Race
Into that northern frontier
These are the journeys
Of the legendary Chupacabra
Its life-long mission:
To continue crossing into that infamous border
Between hard fact and science fiction
To wildly go
Where contemporary lore has never gone before

Miff-ology

Indians don't perform rain dances
Just to rain on your parade
The Easter bunny is not born on Easter
Nor does it give birth to chocolate-covered eggs
St. Valentines may be a propagandist
For porno, failed marriages, happy divorces
St. Nick is truly too fat
To climb down my un-existing chimney
The gleaming tooth fairy
Only visits affluent, popular houses
Not beat-down Mexican barrios
Where the only real truth is that
Chupacabras are rolling down South Luna Street
In supped up Chevys looking for a goat to roll

I Am Chupacabra

I am chupacabra, hear me growl
Through the decades of infamy
Through the media of lies, dark of deception
Through the conversation of who or what is real
Where the media is in fact its own myth

I am chupacabra, hear me growl
At the insanity of death blamed on me
At the ghosts of witnesses pointing their finger the other way
Where rouge restaurants and coyotes are to blame
For a painted, bloody landscaped framed around me

I am chupacabra, hear me growl
At classical mythology and urban myths
Whose proposal of me is non-existential
Whose proponents deny a rightful throne
To me, my one and only true character

I am chupacabra, hear me growl
With the anger of pre-Columbian culture
That perpetuates its mystical figures, their Lloronas
Their mixed, non-conflicting, Christian-paganism
Their bronze-colored Virgin De Guadalupe

I am chupacabra, hear me growl
For it may be the last time in your history
For it threatens to kick me out of the already sick gate
Where many other creatures are denied immigration
Into the land of that great, sweet promise of imagination

I am chupacabra, hear me growl

Ancient Wings

O men of Easter
O Tangata manu
Where we once soared
Like birds in ancient skies
In crowded flocks
About our business
Above solid earth
Where dreams surely cast
Long shadows on grounded men

O men of Easter
O ancient men
Who tore your wings
Off your happy backs
Like the snake, made to slither
On thorny cold floors

O men of Easter
O Rapa Nui
Where we once soared
Like birds through blue skies
Until holy men arrived
Proclaiming that only their God could fly

The Ballad Of The Brazen Ufologist

I
Stand alone, mocked and branded
Like a comic book character
Surrounded by the public in shock and disbelief
Marked, yet brilliant

I
Daring the story be told
One that horrifies our secrecies
Leaves emptiness to understanding
Floats on shiny silver discs
Boldly in the open sky

I
The esoteric scientist attempting to bring to light
Otherworldly beasts and un-human things
To another whose own humanity
Lies terribly in question

I
The brazen ufologist fighting for the truth
…if anyone has any left

Opinionated

She was beautiful as celestial candy goes
As for opinions, like another set of arms
Out in space, everyone has them
With gravity boots on, walked into Space Saloon Seven
Even though she worked there, she asked me for a drink
Turning to the barkeep, noticing his bottom set of arms
No matter what quadrant you think you come from
It just doesn't look right on the guys
Repugnancy aside, I ordered her a Mercury margarita
She soon had me eating out of all four of her lovely hands
As planets revolved their suns, invited myself to her room
Hoping to uncover my personal, heavenly stars
Deception hard at work, soon discovered her second mouth
As for cosmic experiences, this was surely a first

Walking Around The Compound On My Day Off

Sunday walking, slowly, peacefully
Watching the ancient dust settle
After every, heavy, human footstep
Kicking a stone or two on the way
Thinking of the failure of promises
The fantastic idea that 1999* would bring
Yet never really did until years later, now
Thinking of my gorgeous girl back on earth
Hoping she is looking up to her lucky stars
We are that tomorrow, after the shuttles stopped
And tomorrow we head back to the mines
They say there is breathable air to be found there
Harking back to far-fetched fairy tales
Of an old time of active life here on the moon
Like the conniption that man could one day fly
It is what man does to accept the inevitable truth

*The Futuristic TV Show "Space 1999"

Interstellar Drunk

Wanting to drink the stars with human lips
A sip of strong Mercury Margaritas
Another of Jupiter Jack and Coke
Perhaps a Dirty Uranus Low-gravity Ice Tea
An especially frigid Piña Pluto Colada
Maybe Venus Vodka, a Saturn Shooter
Sweet Neptune Nectar, a dry Martian Martini
Too blissfully many cosmic combinations
Still sure there is plenty more
Hopelessly in love with spacial spirits
Helplessly stranded on this common earth
Waiting to taste the heavens on human lips

Pumpkins Despair

Pumpkins grin in their despair
Of hallows eve upon the air
Smell of candlefire within their eye
Hopelessly watching costumes go by

Candy corn dreams of legs and arms
Since birth upon their former farms
So they could shift from present state
To knock on doors and replicate

Yet all they can is sit and wait
Patiently forward with plenty faith
For an October night turned upside down
For despair to break silence to sound

The Cemetery Caretaker

Deep in the sweet silence of the dark night
Is when the constant moaning begins
Sometimes this job does not pay enough

To be awaken from so profound a precious sleep
But one puts up with it if he really cares
For someone must constantly watch over

Those dear, dearly departed
Where rarely relatives come to visit
Somebody must maintain this restful place

There's Dorothy, crying for her children
Her last words from the electric chair
Ten final years after she drowned them

There's Robert never satisfied
Not even after his seventh rape victim
Left a hole between his ogling eyes

There's Jenny always complaining
Needing a clean dressing for her wrists
After being cut out from a relationship

There's John, a complete pervert
Who had an entire lynch mob agreeing
That there was no worse than him

There's Rachel, what a flirt
Who liked to play with drugs and traffic
Who knows where she was going

As for me, I was never a people-person
So I lit up an entire apartment building
Just to prove my point

That's how I got this job
That's how I came to care
That and whatever they fax me from hell

Vanity

Reflecting off the slicing, shiny blade
A lasting beautiful image of me
A lovely, screaming portrait of me
An enduring, haunting memory of me
Death be so kind, un-blind
Dying with a sparkling smile
So that crime-scene snapshots
Permeate my photogenicy
Explaining not who did me wrong
But about how good I look dead

Red Is The Barn

Red is the barn
Like heavy stains upon the floor
Near heaps of lifeless bodies
Of the old farmer and his kin

Red is the barn
That had seen without eyes
The full fury of deep evil
That took life without remorse

Red is the barn
Like the pupils of the aggressor
That lurks amongst the heavy hay
Like the animals that live within

Red is the barn
That does not favor peace
Nor houses such tranquility
But the silence of final death

Red is the barn
Where the truth is hard to swallow
Like a hatchet to the throat
Like red forever to a barn

Waiting

Mother

She was waiting for me
Behind the old, screen door
Wearing a funny, sunny smile

One hand behind her back
Saying she had something special for me
That's my mom

Walking in is when I noticed
Another person inside
On the crimson-covered floor

It's when I noticed
The unsatisfied, swinging ax

It's when I noticed
The blood trickling

Down
    Down
        Down

My fragmenting, foolish face
Forcing a final reflection

Mother… She was waiting for me

Requiem For Satan

For Joe R. Lansdale… respectfully

There in the dark, piney woods
Of a forgotten place in Texas
The beast moves like the hot wind
Heavy, pushing this tree or that
Snapping branches like saltine crackers
Collecting souls with every move
Surely he is looking for me, yet why
Smiling, pointy fangs; smacking his lips
Singing softly, *"Hope you guess my name"*
Or was it the dead radio from the abandoned car
Somehow I think I know what is going on
Dropping the bloody knife, I am sure of it
Agreeing are the lifeless bodies at my feet
"Pleased to meet you, hope you guess my name"

Full Moon Love

Michelle laid perfectly still
As an ancient moon watched from above
Through scattered, dried pine trees

Her perfect, full breasts stared back
Like a large pair of beautiful eyes
Daring never to blink again

The beast smiled roughly like any beast could
Drunken spit, seamen and blood
Splattered about her naked, dead body

Love is what you make of it
They say around these parts of the woods
Where the Red River runs free

Dennis was one of the good guys
Quiet, married, paid his taxes on time
Even wrote a few books in hopes to pay the bills

But where there was a lot of alcohol
Fast women and full moons
All damn bets were off

Waide Aaron Riddle

Waide Aaron Riddle

was born in Kingsville and raised in Houston, Texas. He is the winner of eight national poetry awards and is the author of the critically acclaimed children's story The Chocolate Man: A Children's Horror Tale.

UCLA Library of Special Collections, The Simon Wiesenthal Library/Museum of Tolerance in Beverly Hills and the ONE Institute at USC Los Angeles have archived many of his literary works and poems. The authors who have most inspired Waide are Robert R. McCammon, S.E. Hinton, William Peter Blatty and Dean R. Koontz. In the 1970s, as a boy, he loved reading Famous Monsters of Filmland and was an avid listener of CBS Radio Mystery Theatre. He was also influenced by the great storytellers Vincent Price, Alistair Cooke, Sebastion Cabot and E.G. Marshall.

Mr. Riddle is also an independent filmmaker. His films have screened at numerous film festivals including Cannes Film Festival, Palm Springs International ShortFest and Fort Lauderdale International Film Festival.

When Waide is not writing or shooting a film, he loves to DJ in Los Angeles and Austin dance clubs. His 'library of music' consists of Classic Rock, Today's Country and Golden Oldies.

He can be reached at waideriddle@hotmail.com.

About His Poems:

Potions, Potions, Potions is appearing here for the first time anywhere.

The Court Jester is archived in the **UCLA Library of Special Collections** (2012).

The Wedding Of The Dead previously appeared in the *NOHO Valley News* (1997), *4Front Magazine* (1997), the *California State Poetry Society/Poetry Letter* (2008), and is archived in the **UCLA Library of Special Collections** (2012).

Blackraven previously appeared in the *California State Poetry Society Poetry Letter* (2002) and is archived in **Poet's House/New York City** (2010) and the **UCLA Library of Special Collections** (2011).

Something Wicked Dwells previously appeared in *The HorrorZine.Com* (2012), The *Horror Zine Summer Digest 2012*, and is archived in the **UCLA Library of Special Collections** (2012).

Handsome is archived in the **UCLA Library of Special Collections** (2012).

Dinner Tonight... With Friends previously appeared in *The HorrorZine.Com* (2012) and *The Horror Zine Summer Digest 2012*.

Ghost Tellers is archived in the **UCLA Library of Special Collections** (2012).

Dark Circus is archived in the **UCLA Library of Special Collections** (2012).

The Dance Of The Ghosts previously appeared in the *NOHO Valley News* (1997), *4Front Magazine* (1996), and is archived in the **UCLA Library of Special Collections** (2011).

A Haunting In Arkansas/The Evil Evening previously appeared in *The HorrorZine.Com* (2012), *The Horror Zine Summer Digest 2012*, and is archived in the **UCLA Library of Special Collections** (2012).

31 October Street previously appeared in the *NOHO Valley News* (1997), *4Front Magazine* (1997), and is archived in the **UCLA Library of Special Collections** (2012).

The Halloween Lullaby previously appeared in the *NOHO Valley News* (1997) and *4Front Magazine* (1997).

Auschwitz previously appeared in the online anthology *Poetry Super Highway's Holocaust Remembrance Day 2015*.

Bayou's Hex is appearing here for the first time anywhere.

Jack O' Lantern Fever previously appeared in *4Front Magazine* (1996).

Beautiful Blue previously appeared in the chapbook, *All-American Texan* (1999).

Beginner's Spell is appearing here for the first time anywhere.

Excerpt From The Poem: "The Chocolate Man: A Children's Horror Tale" was officially broadcasted on FM Radio in Louisville, Kentucky and Los Angeles, California in 2002, and it was also live-streamed on KUT in Austin, Texas in 2012.

Black Night previously appeared in the chapbook, *All-American Texan* (1999).

Potions, Potions, Potions

Let me present my potions to you.
Some are very old and some are quite new.
Some apply like black oil
And others have a fragrance of a sweet fine oil.

Potions, potions, potions

All homemade by me! See?
I can make potions to curse, and to bless and to test one's love.

Potions, potions, potions

A little of this and a little of that.
An eye of a bat. A furry tail of a cat. A tooth of a rat.
A needle and thread...
A token to exercise one's skill to kill.

Potions, potions, potions

Gracious me! What have I made here?
A gift of a doll to you... Isn't it clear?

Potions, potions, potions

Ahhh... as the garlic is to the vampire.
As Wolf's Bane is to the werewolf.
As blood lust is to both, let me cast you a spell
And I'm only happy to send your enemy to Hell.

Potions, potions, potions

Trinkets and bottles of lotions
And full of who knows what?
'Careful there of those broken edges...
Oh, they'll cut.

Potions, potions, potions

Witchcraft and ghostly ghouls and doctors of voodoo.
Demonic possession, oh, who knew?
Do I have just the right concoction for you?
You bet I do!

Potion, potions, potions

Exotic. Erotic. Hypnotic. Psychotic.
Something for everyone. Something for every taste.
Something for every human case.

Potions, potions, potions

Onward I go. High and low.
To my next stop, whether or not
My potions be for the lost... or not.

The Court Jester

The act begins. The Court Jester bows.
The jester's gesture wins applause from the crowd.
SILENCE!! Motions his Highness...

Bells, bangles & baubles

Trinkets for the wealthy and royal snobs.
Tall tales and comedy skits and jokes for the village folks.
He swears he's no hoax. Tricks with a mix of acrobatic kicks.
He has their attention!
He insists his mysteries are of the non-fiction.
The King is so pleased as the Queen smiles with uneasy ease.

A glittery costume of shiny tassels

He tells of the legends of dragons and magic castles.
A sudden spin and he's a flashy blur.
A whir that startles his audience.

...purples and blues...orange and yellow hues...
...violets and pinks...fire and ice colors...
...a spectral marvel hovered...
...a gleam and sheen of blinding red and green...
...rainbow smoke...a billow of crimson fire came...
...which turned into a cobalt flame...

Commoners and royalty scream at his game.
The act is finished. The jester vanished.
The crowd roars with pleasure
At the royal Christmas gift that is such a treasure.
The village musicians and minstrels break into a musical ditty.
The masquerade and charade is over. What a pity!
Now, let the holiday dance begin,
As the kingdom's choir sings in...

"What a merry ole' time it has been!"
"Cheers to the Court Jester!"
"For it is he who has won us again!"

The Wedding Of The Dead

The time has come for the Wedding,
The Wedding of the Dead.
Ring the *bells* and strike the *chimes*!
Celebrate the Day of All Saints.
The Wedding welcomes you.
The Bride of Death in black lace and veils.
Black roses adorn her bridesmaids.
The Groom of Death holds the traditional black rose ring
And the church is full of the *smiling dead...*
The Wedding welcomes you.
Bats. Vultures. Crows. Ravens.
They circle the church and the cemetery grounds.
Goons, ghouls, freaks, banshees and zombies crowd the church.
The Bride walks the aisle.
The Wedding welcomes you.
Bride and Groom smile... faces black with rotted teeth...
Each say, *"I do..."* and *"I love you, too."*
Time to celebrate this ancient tradition.
The Wedding welcomes you.
The Wedding of the Dead.
Evening approaches and darkness paints the world.
The guests and ghosts of the past raise their glasses...
"Let's make a toast with this fine red wine.
To The Day of All Saints!"
The Wedding welcomes you.

Blackraven

Enter into night
in this house
of dark and no light.

Where Evil lives
and ghosts and specters remember...
and never forgive.

This house known as Blackraven,
haunted by Death, where there is no God...
There is no Heaven.

Something Wicked Dwells

Haunted this house is. Gravely old.
Full of danger. Full of darkness.
Death... and *evil*.
Lurking room to room.
Slithering from stair to stair.
From attic to basement. Hidden chambers.
Lying in wait... for me.
It is my Master. Is it all in my head?
Am I insane?
Am I mad?
Listen... can't you hear him?
The voices... His demonic yells.
Something wicked dwells.
The spirits and specters... they foretell the spells
Of the forthcoming hell.
Beware.
They tell me of each toll of the bell.
A ghost will tell the tales of this house.
Immortal.
A mere warning to me...
A mortal.
Something wicked dwells beyond these bolted doors.
Closer, it comes.
Closer.
Louder I yell-
Who's there? Good God I fear you!
I feel it. Everywhere. Surrounding me. Covering me.
But, my eyes lie to me... Nothing anywhere...

But, I know *It's* there. *He's* there.
Something wicked dwells.
The evil roaming... *He* is roaming.
In this house, where something wicked dwells.

Handsome

Midnight in the Victorian homestead.
Sneaking through a window, nearly bumping my head.
Thankfully I didn't, so, I forged ahead.
Every room with candlelight... a gothic rainy night...
It was only I and the rainfall outside. A sudden dank chill...
I allowed myself a sigh.
Candle in hand, cautiously, roaming the halls.
A thunder outside, as if a warning call,
Stone and brick surrounded me,
Whispers in the darkness ahead... movement?
I'm sure of it! I just can't see.
I push open a creaking wooden door
Hoping for treasures to be in store.
My luck!
Wall to wall paintings galore.
I began looking... Fascinated... entranced...
How beautiful the art and all by hand.
The prospects suddenly enhanced...
"Hello," came a voice that whispered behind me.
In a start, I spun to see who had alarmed me.
And there he was, the most handsome man in the world.
The chill turned to sudden cold.
His face illuminated by candle glow.
He said, *"Welcome to my home."*
I was speechless through to the bone.
I stood stone still not knowing what to do.
That's when I detected the hypnotic scent of his cologne.
His skin was olive. His hair an ink black...

And so was the cat that scurried past my feet,
Arching its back... hissing... as if to attack.
The man smiled... and I know...
I saw a glint of a sharp tooth.
Common sense told me that this time
I'd probably made a major goof.
He said, *"My name is Luciano. Please, stay. Don't go...*
For it's just started. The show!"
His speech was articulate and eloquent.
An attitude obscenely debonair.
But, it was his stare that spoke of individual savior- faire.
Luciano was refined. Those luscious lips outlined.
And those teeth! Frighteningly defined.
He was striking and was so well groomed from head to toe.
Locked in his eyes, the image of a crimson moon.
He was tailored in a fine classic tuxedo, with white gloves,
Saying humorously, *"Glad you're taken with my paintings...*
which you obviously love."
He held me in a waltz stance. Such the Casanova!
Turn! Step! Dance! Dance! Dance!
Falling deeper into his sensual trance.
As we slowed to a still, my heart beat to the thrill.
"Your lips... I'd kill for a kiss..."
... How poetic, Luciano... My first thought... No pun there.
Should I run? Do I dare?
He said, *"Don't even think about it. Don't you dare."*
His lips opened over my lips.
Thoughts of fire and unearthly desires.
He sighed into me.
His breath feeding me.
His lips moved gracefully over my face, to my neck...

The breath hot... the lips moist.
I knew I was his next.
He held my face in a lovers' clasp.
A dead cold wind blew the candles to black.
In the darkness, I knew it was over.
As Luciano fed, in the safety of the rooms darkness,
And this night's eternal cover.

Dinner Tonight... With Friends

The fly eats mud.
The fly eats crud.
Rotted flesh... mmm... smells mighty yummy!
An open sore. What a fantasy!
The fly says "Hi!"
Garbage is good for dessert.
The fly burrows and breeds... larva... ooze... goo...
The fly and the watermelon. Sweet treat.
Almost better than dog meat.
The fly is happy.
Dinner tonight with friends.
Roaches and maggots... have such appetites!

Ghost Tellers

We are the Ghost Tellers meeting night after night.
Sometimes by candle light.
All the better on cold cloudy rainy nights.
We tell the stories that frighten and thrill
And always happy to instill feelings of the macabre.
All the better to make your heart pound and throb.
Bathing your senses in oceans of unknown emotions.

Relax...remember the Boogey Man?
Don't lie, of course, everyone can.
When was the last time you looked under your bed?
Think you'd rather face the thud in the darkened closet instead?

The clock strikes midnight.
It is the hour. Don't be a coward and cower.
It's only as real as you make it.

Sit.
Forget...the real world's problems,
For the Ghost Tellers can't solve them.
But, we'll take you on a journey into fun.
Away from your life of carried strife and glum.
Like a grave robber in a cemetery,
Not even we know what he'll unearth...
Perhaps the Grim Reaper...who carries the death curse.

We are the Ghost Tellers.
Now that the mood is set,
We hope your expectations will fully be met.
On this Gothic night,
Let the Ghost Tellers open their books to near abandon light...
Sharing with you the world of many frights.

Dark Circus

Every Christmas, traveling from tomb to town,
Under a night sky of blue and red stars...
"Welcome to the Dark Circus, ladies and gentlemen..."
The Ring Master greets you in black and white,
Like a vampire dressed for the night.
"There he is, the hunch back court jester,
Made up in silver and gold and red,
You'd swear he's already dead! Wouldn't you?
Meet Ivan, the handsome juggler.
Possessing eyes as blue as the winter moon.
And the ugly old hag,
With a bag full of glittered black *Devil's Dust*.
Oh, she's a must for all to see.
Please welcome the gypsies and minstrels...
They will gladly take your donation
While our beautiful Asian magician
Seduces you with her hypnotic levitation.
Now we warn you... cover your children's eyes...
For the Dark Circus does not lie...
Prepare yourself! Silence please...Silence...
Yes... Be at ease. Enter now...
Let the ghosts of thirteen naked dancing men surround you...
Lose yourself.
Gladiators, warriors, slaves of ancient Rome...
Actual *real* ghosts of a time passed,
Alas, the Dark Circus is their only home.
Set your eyes upon them.
Such beauty in their nudity as they caress each other.

A dance that is art. Masculine touching masculine.
Dancing in waves of sodomy and oral pleasures
That only tongue and lips can treasure.
Ah. Yes, the audience is in shock!
Ha, only the timid will walk...
Well, let them!"
The Dark Circus will leave you with a devil's smile.
The blue and red night is drawing to a close,
It's just about through,
The Ring Master tips his hat and says,
"Merry Christmas to you!"

The Dance Of The Ghosts

Dark...Eternal...Entombed
BANG! CLANG!
Souls of the decade. Centuries.
Muffled whispers...Laughing shadows
CRACKLE! TAP! TAP! CLICK!
Banshees scream
Wind. Fog. Mists swirl...
Twilight melts into night.
POP! CHANTS! BUMP! SNAP!
Cryptic creaks
The mausoleum is alive...BANG!
The cemetery lives
The old dark house vibrates
Claps of deafening thunder
It's music to their ears
Lightening snakes and shears
Rain...
THUMPS! CRASH!
Ding dong... The chime of midnight
Ding dong... OOOH... It has begun...
The dance of the ghosts

A Haunting In Arkansas/The Evil Evening

Earthen colors crept over the Arkansas landscape.
Muted shadows overlapped shadows.
A melancholy painting...
An overcast sky of brush strokes haunted the winters day.
Fall was dead and buried.
Blacks. Grays. Drabs. Blahs...
Melted like wax into the soil of the countryside.
Devils' fingers decorated each tree limb
With withered leaves and burnt bark.
Slits in the overcast stung the lull
In red and orange afternoon sunray.
Specters breath blew cold upon frozen lakes and ponds.
This, in return, roused the night creatures
And hunger and thirst followed.
Howls in a distant hollow...
The forest went from mud brown to murky black.
The creeper crept... unseen... whisper like...
Throughout the wicked willows...
A snap of a twig.
A doe startled... then pranced away with her young.
Shades are drawn.
Doors are locked.
Spiders race toward web vibrations in the dark cellars.
Mold is the perfume of the night.
Again...howls in a distant hollow.

31 October Street

I will never forget the house...
Deep in the black wood...
Down the fog swept dirt road...
'Cross the moaning swaying bridge...
The house at 31 October Street.

The legend is alive and well.
Secrets I dare not tell.
Smeared with the blood of foolish hosts.
Haunted by hungry ghosts.
The house at 31 October Street.

A bastion of hallways, passageways and secret rooms.
Trap doors that lead you to a grisly doom.
"In the name of God..." A priest shall nod.
"Save the soul of the one who enters."
The house at 31 October Street.

The grounds are cursed.
The evil lurks.
Fear it. Beware of it. Never forget it.
The stories and tales that fill this lost dead street...
There! You've come upon it!
The house at 31 October Street.

The Halloween Lullaby

GHOSTS, GHOULS, GOBLINS
Deep in the gallows
Share in the madness and fun...children do.
Adults, too!
Celebrate! It's a holiday! A festive one, yet
It's the Halloween Lullaby!
WITCHES, WARLOCKS, NOSFERATU, QUASIMODO, too
Don't be shy, sing along the 31st Lullaby
Black cats. Black bats.
Owls go *'whooo...'* Ghosts go *'booo...'*
Specters, spirits, trick or treat
Lots of candy and lots of fun
Pumpkin patch, pumpkin pie
It's all in fun- couldn't you just die?!
Celebrate! Time to dance! Time to party!
There's a Wolf-man. There's a Vampire.
C'mon, time to build a cozy fire
Let's bob for apples
Light some candles
Spooky shadows in the cemetery
Séance madness and Ouija Board fever
It's just for fun, so boogie some
It's the Halloween Lullaby!
Halloween Lullaby!

Auschwitz

Cold and worn, I sit crouched in the corner of the train.
My clothes and hopes are torn, too.
Gloom paints my mind. God has turned blind.
In the snow there is death and stain.
Cold winds sting...I shiver to sleep.
Silence.
My family and friends huddle close. As the train stops...slowly.
I peer outside. Lanterns and lights lit.
I see the sign and I shudder:

"Welcome To Auschwitz"

I am separated. Insulted. Harassed. Humiliated.
Branded with a pink triangle.
I close my eyes hoping to be taken away by my guardian angel.
I am led to a small prison- like hole.
Others like me, their spirits stole.
Gaunt. Starved. Rot and poison, forced to eat.
The guards take me down. Hold me to the ground.
They spit. They rape me... laughing,
"You queer kike. We know you like!"
They all take turns. My friends watch in a trance,
Others prefer to shut their eyes, only to periodically glance.
The German Nazi bastards!
They have made a theatrics of me.
Day after day. One by one. My friends disappear...
With tears in my eyes I fear.
I am so thin I can barely stand. Weak.

They're trying to kill me. I pray them to be damned.
Today is gray.
The world is snowing and moaning.
Led one by one we are stripped.
The moment terrifying, insanity fully gripped.
Naked.
Then commanded to run.
For them it's all fun.
Suddenly they aim their guns.
I don't look back on this mounting attack.
Shots are fired. Bodies collapse.
I am so slow. My feet numb.
I give myself up, body and soul.
My wasted body falls with a thud in the snow.
I can no longer move.
How I long to feel my mother's hands sooth.
A boot stomps my face. Blood I taste.
The snow is splattered. The flesh on my face tattered.
For an instant, in my mind, I see my family separated from me.
I watched them ushered into the showers.
Doors close. Screams. Agony.
I could do nothing.
The stench of their deaths absorbed in my skin.
An omen. Soon coming.
Cold.
Ice fills my mouth.
My eyes no longer can shut.
The black seeping. And surrounding.
The pain in my body released.
Death becoming.

Bayou's Hex

Moss was tossed into the swamp.
The Voodoo Master stirred in a slow motion.
Thus finished the potion.
A witch cackles and yells in delight.
For the dark spell foretells what's in for the night.

The *Hoodoo Tavern* was a pub
That sat deep within the bayou's grassy hubs.
Out of the way. Miles away.
The *Hoodoo Tavern,*
Like a cavern inside, lit with fire lamps.
The hillbilly music played,
As the fiddle players stamped their feet,
In the humid damp heat.

REX...swayed in the smoky haze...
He was a native to the marsh.
He had learned to live with its harsh ways.
Rex was 'inbred', you can tell.
Hell, it did something funny in his head.
You'd swear sometimes he'd be the living dead.
Foolin' around with his Ma and brothers in the shack's bed.

Rex was taken with the strings.
Oh, how his head would sing.
His body jerked.
The crow alert and watched, caught by this change in Rex.
The bayou's hex.

A backwoods spell.
Outside the zombies hide.
Covens of banshees yell.
"Go to Hell!"

Rex was the color of dark bone.
Sun-stained skin with the blend of mocha.
His long hair was the black of the widow.
A stuffed crow nailed against the wall.
It's eyes, beady glass, saw it all.
Caw Caw Caw it seemed to warn.

Rex's eyes were serpentine green.
They pulsed and glowed and beamed.
So it seemed.
Wearing only faded jeans, his body coiled serpentine.
Moving slowly, twisting.
Deep within his throat a ghostly hissing.
The folk watched in anticipation.
They were all, after all, family relation.

His mouth opened…
And a tongue flicked and licked out and about.
A forked gray tongue.
The hex stung.

Rex made a strike.
His bite would be fatal.
Two venomous fangs hang over his lower lip.
The transition was complete, in the bayou's night heat.
The spell complete. Rex joined his family of snakes.
The out-of-towners would be his bait.
One after the other would meet their fate.
Outside, there was a full moon.
The undead restless in the mosquito drenched gloom.
The bayou's hex foreshadowed and loomed.
Rex would be among them, sealing a stranger's doom.

Jack O' Lantern Fever

Tick...Tock...chimes the old clock
It's midnight, time to fire the night
Strike the match
Crimson orange light
Pumpkin bright.
So thick, you can slice it with a knife
Jagged teeth and scary eyes
How about a piece of pumpkin pie!?
Mystical. Magical. Ancient and phenomenal.
Celebrate and participate in this Halloween ritual
Eerie...Creepy...Ghoulish fun
In the pumpkin patch, round the bon fire, near the cemetery...
Hey, that's where it's at!
Grab a white sheet, hold your pumpkin tight,
'Cause I hear it's gonna be a bumpy night!
Don't take it seriously, have a little fun
That's what it's about
'Cause if you don't, we'll just have to kick you out!

Beautiful Blue

When I look into your eyes
I see a summer rain...
Falling on an ocean...
Sunlight shimmering through
      Cloud...
                      Raindrops...
    ...Glistening....

Beginner's Spell

Rage of water...the anger of fire.
The eye of a specter...winds that cut and voices that tempt.
Secrets that are kept.
Night creatures of the forest...crawlers of caves.
Phantoms that breathe...while roaches and maggots breed.
Death of an angel. Dark Lord lead me.
Volcano and thunder...lava orange...
Stone and rock. Marble cold.
Steel walls enslave.
White witch hear me...ancient power.
Black witch speak to me...ancient rite.
Covens and Warlocks show yourselves now!
Come to me. Ride the midnight winds...
Come to me. I...am yours...

Excerpt From The Poem:
"The Chocolate Man: A Children's Horror Tale"

Deep in the belly of Blackraven,
Within the tributaries of its caverns,
Dean sat on the floor chained.
An orange-skinned girl sat arranged next to him.
She had only one arm.
He could see she was emotionally maimed.
How pitiful, what a shame, he thought.
Almost beyond fear and its tears, Dean was torn.
Flies swarmed to the sound of the storm outside.
She cried to herself.
He wanted to cry for her.
He wanted to die at this sight,
In the shadows,
Where they were,
Where there was very little light.

"What happened?" he asked, trying to mask his feelings.

After a moment she whispered, "He ate it."

"I'm sorry," Dean, said back, speechless,
For the proper words he lacked.

"He said I tasted like pumpkin pie."
And then she sighed as a fly buzzed by.
"I'm going to die."

"No, you won't and I'm not going to let him hurt you anymore, for that is my promise."

"Thank you…My name is Jean."

"I'm Dean."

And for a moment there was a gleam of hope in both their eyes.

"They were before us," Jean said.

The cavern cell felt as warm with ghosts.
The floor strewn with bones and remains of the candy man's victims.

"Listen. You can hear them."

The stench stank.
It crawled high and lowly deep.
It seeped here and there and everywhere.
This stink of rot caught cryptic drafts and breeze.
There was dis-ease in the moans and groans and cries
and sighs and chants and rants and mourning and warning
in the sounds of the dead.
Ghosts that showed themselves in white-blue transparent shadows.
Specters and phantoms that haunt and taunt
Wafted by and high in a macabre phantasmagoria dance.
Wall to wall, tall and small,
Claws in the wall, fall in a slow motion fall,
Jean and Dean saw as the apparitions spun and twirled,

floated and rotated, inflated and deflated,
Hung and lunged to and fro and about.
Dean and Jean watched in wonder
as the thunder thundered outside.
Too late to hide.
The door of some unknown cold chasm had been unlocked . . .
This was real. . .
No phantasm.

He was, has and will always be evil.
A bad seed of bad deeds.
A mother and father who bore a monster.
A twist of fate.
A caller who crept under the gates of another place and time.
A place with no map.
A time with no existence.
A trickster. A prankster.
A clown of the night made up in black and white.

"Lollipops, lollipops
Tops that spin and hop.
Kids love candy
My sugar is poison, it sure is dandy.
Try a sip of my candied brandy
With my candied dandies."

Season after season the reason remains a mystery.
A history of mystery.
He succeeds in his deeds.
Planting the seeds that lead to the end.
Never to mend.

"Why," said the fly, "should they die?"

His mask is powerful.
To remove it takes special task.
Now, aren't you glad you asked?
Listen up carefully . . .
There is no answer, unfortunately, for something that just is.
End of quiz.

Black Night

Earth brown eyes...Butterscotch castles...Raven black hair...
Ride the wings of stars on a crystal black night.
A smile so beautiful...As beautiful as Heaven.

Rie Sheridan Rose

Rie Sheridan Rose lives

in Texas with her husband Newell and a small herd of cat babies. Since she was a little girl, her goal has always been to be a writer—along with an archaeologist, a detective, an actress, and several other dreams that fell by the wayside. The writing is the only goal that stayed constant. She has been writing professionally all century. In that time, she has written six novels, five poetry chapbooks, and numerous short stories. Her stories appear in *Come to My Window, In the Bloodstream, The Grotesquerie, Nightmare Stalkers and Dream Walkers, Shifters*, and several other anthologies. Her poetry has appeared in *Metastasis, Di-Verse-City, Bones II, Twenty: Poems in Memoriam* to name a few. Yard Dog Press is home to her humorous horror chapbooks *Tales from the Home for Wayward Spirits and Bar-B-Que Grill* and *Bruce and Roxanne Save the World...Again*, which will soon be collected in a perfect-bound edition. Mocha Memoirs has published the individual short stories "Drink My Soul...Please," and "Bloody Rain" as e-downloads. She also collaborated with Marc Gunn on lyrics for his **"Don't Go Drinking With Hobbits"** CD as well as some individual pieces. Melange Books carries her romantic fantasy *Sidhe Moved Through the Faire*. Zumaya Books is home to *The Luckless Prince* as well as her newest novel, *The Marvelous Mechanical Man*. Her other novels are out-of-print at the moment.

About Her Poems:

Sibling Rivalry previously appeared in *Mythic Circle* and *Straying From The Path.*

Chains Of Straw—Ropes Of Gold previously appeared on the ShadowKeep website.

Down In The Hollow previously appeared in *By Candlenight.*

My Boyfriend's Dead previously appeared in *Take Out From the Writer's Café.*

A Treatise On Spell Components previously appeared in *By Candlelight.*

By Candlelight previously appeared in *Aberrant Dreams* and *By Candlelight.*

Best Be Ware previously appeared in *Abyss & Apex* and *By Candlelight.*

Outdated previously appeared in *Straying From The Path.*

And The Skeletons Will Kick Your Ass previously appeared in *By Candlelight.*

To Tell Medusa No... previously appeared in *Take Out From the Writer's Café.*

Concerning The Burning Of Witches In Salem previously appeared in *Take Out From the Writer's Café.*

Annabel Dawn previously appeared in *Take Out From the Writers Café.*

Raise A Glass In Parting previously appeared on the CD, *Don't Go Drinking With Hobbits,* and in its accompanied songbook.

Ain't That The Way previously appeared in *Dancing on The Edge.*

The Soul Of A Harper previously appeared on the CD, *Brobdingnagian Fairy Tales.*

Midnight Encounter previously appeared in *Dreams Of Decadence* and *If My Sandcastle Drowns... Can I Live with You?*

The Standing Stones previously appeared in *If My Sandcastle Drowns... Can I Live with You?*

Ride The Red Wind previously appeared in *Abandoned Towers.*

The Bridge Of Birds appears here for the first time.

The Starlight Bathing appears here for the first time.

Sibling Rivalry

I

Following the pebbles
through a night
like velvet—

Mother looked at
Gretel
with eyes of
green fire.

it was inevitable
she'd try
again.

and

when the second
chance occurred,
she must
have raked
the courtyard with
a feather
to leave
no stones....

II

In the darkness
of the
ancient trees,
it was
Gretel
who found
a way—

drawn by the
siren call
of
like to like—

and I,
as always,
followed.

III

Gretel
would have
stayed forever.

She was used to the
work,
and gathered stray
spells

in her spare
time.

She would stand
before my cage
and mutter
to herself,
glancing my way
with
a speculative
eye.

        IV

Days flow
like rivers—

swift with
a floodtide
of events
and emotions

or

sluggish with
the ennui
of stagnation.

I lived a
lifetime

behind those
bars,
alone with
thoughts and
sweetmeats.

Gretel
grew strong
as I
grew stale.

I think she even
came to like
the old woman—
witch or no.

          V

I had never
seen my

sister
happy,
until
I was
imprisoned.

She sang
about the
kitchen

as she
made my meals—

and over her
shoulder
loomed the
oven.

She goaded me to join
her songs—

But, being for
the cook pot,

I couldn't take
things as lightly...

and all my
songs were
dirges.

VI

It wasn't easy to
persuade my sister
to her duty.

Her loyalty to kin
was always
loose at

best,
learned as it was
at Mother's knee.

Ambition warred
with what
little love was
left.

Only promised
futures
convinced her
in the end,

not shared pasts.

Left to her
own will,

I think she would
have sucked the
marrow from my bones
like wine.

And left my
skull
for the crows.

Chains Of Straw—
Ropes Of Gold

I

I was happy at the mill.

My part was simple…
it was Father who did the work.

All I need do was
greet the customers,

and lead their eyes
away from the weights
when it was time to
pay.

but Father
had a big mouth
for such a
little man….

II

"My daughter…can spin straw to gold!"

An idle boast
offered over one
too many mugs
of ale—

unfortunately
it was offered
to the wrong
people….

and I wound up
with an underground
address.

III

By royal decree
a room was filled
with a pile of straw
that touched the
ceiling like a
golden waterfall

before it sat a simple wheel
and a three-legged stool
and me.

IV

If Father had had a brain
perhaps he would have
kept his mouth shut…

but we were for it now…

and I stared at the straw and
saw summer fields and
boys with supple tans and

I wept for
days of beauty
remembered.

But tears are easily misinterpreted—

and he thought
I wept for
days of future
lost.

and so he came to me….

…and offered to make things right.

Being in no position to bargain,
I said yes—

but I didn't know the price.

V

If I spin your straw to gold—
save you from this dungeon cold—
bring about your fate foretold—
what, then, shall I get to hold?

There was a wistful laugh behind his words
as he ducked and turned his head away....

a twisted little figure
with the eyes of a
poet....

and so
I gave to him
a ring—

a trifle
won at Forfeits
from a field hand
in the summer straw

and did not see
the awe

with which
he took it.

VI

the king was most impressed.

VII

The next day there were two piles of straw—

one must admire the king's persistence,
even while deploring his greed…

and so I sat again before the golden mountains
and wondered if he'd come.

VIII

Asleep,
I dreamed a handsome prince
drifted past the mill
on a gilded boat
and—catching a glimpse—
came to my side
and brushed
a kiss
across my brow,
murmuring,

"I love thee so…."

In a voice like spring wine.

    IX

Gasping awake,
        to a cell of stone
                with bars of steel
                        I saw him retreat
                                into the shadows

    X

If I can break you from this hold
by spinning all this straw to gold—
swell the kingdom's wealth tenfold—
for what price is my labor sold?

There was something hidden behind those liquid eyes—
swimming in their infinite depths—
it almost broke the surface
before it dove back into his heart.

I gave him
a locket
that had belonged
to my mother

and noted the
ring

upon one lily hand.

    XI

They say third time's the charm.

    XII

The dungeon was now so packed with straw
they barely had a place to set the wheel.

I was suffocating

and yet
I prayed
to see him—

though
I had
but one
gift
left to give….

    XIII

I looked behind me,
and he was there.

perched upon
the heap of straw
and watching

me

with eyes
that gave away
his secrets.

XIV

Here we are as was of old—
you, with straw that must be gold...
I, with hands the secret hold—
what gift shall I now be doled?

the words were soft and
oh...so infinitely sweet—

I looked behind the twisted mask
into the shelter of that hidden heart
and all the walls came crashing down.

I gave to him
the only thing
I had left—

I gave to him a kiss
from my soul
to his

and his hands spun so fast that the gold flowed like a river,
washing me to a throne—

    XV

So here I sit, on my empty throne,
waiting for a child
I both fear and crave….
And I wish I knew his name.

Down In The Hollow

*Jocund day stands tiptoe
on the misty mountaintops…*

But down in the hollow,
the crows stand watch.

They ride the skies,
tattered ebon wraiths
with gemstone eyes of golden fire,
wheeling ash on the wind….

Down in the hollow,
the trees huddle close.

Their skeletal branches
reach for Heaven,
pleading, boney fingers like
the dead importuning….

Down in the hollow,
the wind whispers secrets.

Crying and keening
babbling in tongues

in and out of the writhing trees,
bloodless ghosts….

Down in the hollow,
Grim men live watchful.

They tend their comrades
of wing and twig,
abide the wind's teaching,
and hold their own council.

My Boyfriend's Dead

My boyfriend's dead
and that's such a bummer
He's such a big jerk...
it's just barely summer!

I knew we were screwed
when we went to the park
to fool around on the swings
where it's quiet and dark

and that man-eating ghoul
with the half-melted face
started chewing on Scott
while I dug for my mace.

It was really quite gross
and a terrible curse
'cause I couldn't find anything
down in my purse...

At least that old zombie ate
only Scott's arm
if he'd eaten his face
that would cause more alarm...

'Cause Scott's more a runner
and can't really throw
but he IS quite the looker --
like Matt Damon, y'know?

I know that Scott's dead,
but he's still my Prom date
so I bought some breathmints
and I can't hardly wait

for his rising tonight
'cause I bet there are perks
to a love that's a zombie...
Well, we'll see if this works...

If not, I'll call Peter...

A Treatise On Spell Components
—A. Giant, Wizard

Delicate, tiny,
clutched in my fist,
a handful of fingerbones
snapped at the wrist.

Potions and portents,
spells and what-not...
it isn't so easy
to get what I've got.

Finding a donor
to give you a hand
can be very costly...
the sums they demand!

I find it much easier,
as I grow in my art
just to find a live specimen
and rip it apart.

By Candlelight

The madman drinks
from a silver cup
wrought from a skull
bright dipped.
He sips from wine
laced with blood,
and his thoughts are
mad thoughts.
He braids his
moonlight hair
with the charms
of his youth—
Cat's Cradle tangles
framing the worn map
of his ancient visage.
Behind the shutters
of his ghost-pale eyes
breed monsters and
maniacs.
And the results come
knocking.

Best Be Ware

The marrow bones
rattle
in the wind
tonight—

and on the
vast moor,
something howls....

They say the
Hunt
will ride
tonight—

searching for
souls
to harvest
like grapes.

Best be ware
and lock
the bairns
in the cupboards.

'Tis an
evil wind
that carries
the cry of
the horn

and
all heads
turn
when the
Hunt
rides by.

Outdated

I

A prick from
the spindle—
momentary pain

and dreams
forgotten at
a stranger's

kiss...

my world
was defined
by dreams

crystal clear,
safe,
impenetrable,

slumber
was all
I knew...

II

Have you any idea
how much
things change
in a century?

I am supposed
to be grateful to
the prince who
awakened me,

but everything
we ever knew
is dead.

Countries rose
and fell
to dust
around us—

my kingdom
shrank to our doorstep
as we slept,

and the brambles
were cleared
for souvenirs.

III

He speaks casually
of things
I've never heard of—
this noble rescuer
of mine—
and laughs
in my face
at my ignorance

"What, you've never heard of—?"
"You've never seen a—?"
"Girl, where have you been?!"
knowing full well.

He promises
I'll grow accustomed
to his new
world...

but even Father weeps.

And The Skeletons Will Kick Your Ass

If you go a-hunting
where you shouldn't be
for things you mustn't know…
then watch your way
when the Hunt goes by
and keep your head down low.

For if you wander in parts unknown
and unknowable by men…
the skeletons will kick your ass
for messing with their kin.

They are silver and silent
beneath the moon
and run together in
like roving wolves with packs—
swords for fangs
and rags upon their backs.

The watchhounds of the underworld
thousands on thousands they run…
but if you survive till break of day—
they vanish when kissed by sun.

To Tell Medusa No...

If I were looking for a quick release
from the game of life,
I would tell the Gorgon to her face
and spend eternity forever poised
and perfect...
never aging, never dying...at least in the messy sense.

But I am more coward than
courageous,
and foolish enough to
dream tomorrow better...
so no.

Not in person, then.

Perhaps I could send a note—
entrusted to one I despise,
and kill two birds with one...stone...
as it were.

But I would like be named
for the crime,
and prison is so confining...
so no.

Does Medusa have a telephone,
out there on her lonely rock?
Surrounded by the indifferent sea

and lots of statuesque fish?
Her bills would be outrageous—
and I doubt she'd accept collect...
so no.

An email, routed through the
safety of the Internet?
But who could guess her username...
Olsnakehead3 is probably not a safe bet...
so no.

I suppose I must shout my defiance
to the wind.
"No! No! A million times, no!"
And hope one breath of insolence
is carried to her lonely ear.

Concerning The Burning Of Witches In Salem

I stand here on this
windy hilltop—
insubstantial as smoke...
but not from flames.

I was there
and I know

The children were bored
they were caught
at things
they were not meant
to play...

so they lied

and we died

but not to fire,
the heat of flame,
the pain of the burning
bones melting into
charred dust—

our deaths were cold.

That poor old man—Giles Corey—
who refused to confess

a sin he did not own...
and was crushed to death
'neath a pile of stone.

Sweet, daft Sarah...
a handful of others...
dead in prison
from the privations
and the pain.

And the rest of us
the nineteen who share
this hill
drifting like the
myth of smoke

we hung from their ropes
breath choking our
prayers to Heaven
and we swung
like the pendulum
that has forgotten
the truth.

Annabel Dawn

Wispy clouds flitting across the moon, giving me the shivers...
I peer through shadows of the night, ghost ships haunt the rivers.

I seek for someone that was lost, who rode before the mast...
I fear he comes not home to me, that life for him is past.

Oh, Johnny, why'd ye go from me?
Oh, Johnny, why'd ye stray?
Oh, Johnny, come ye home to me—
to sail another day.

The night it is so cold and grey, the mist like ghost hands plays
I cannot see the way to go...the path—I think it strays!

They said the ship had come to dock, but one man left aboard
No one would tell me who he was, not for a treasure hoard.

Oh, Johnny, why'd ye go from me?
Oh, Johnny, why'd ye stray?
Oh, Johnny, come ye home to me—
to sail another day.

And so I go to seek myself, the truth of what occurred.
I'll take no heed of friend or foe, and heed only his word.

But the way is cold and damp, and I fear that I am lost
The path it crumbles underfoot—to the current I am tossed...

Oh, Johnny, why'd ye go from me?
Oh, Johnny, why'd ye stray?
Oh, Johnny, come ye home to me—
to sail another day.

My gown is heavy now with damp, the water pulls me down...
My last thought is again of John, as in its arms I drown.

I peer though shadows of the night, ghost ships haunt the rivers.
Wispy clouds flitting across the moon, giving me the shivers...

Raise A Glass In Parting

The time will come for leaving…
I know you cannot stay
But later for the grieving…
You're here with me today.

I'd rather tend my garden
Than wander down the road
And so, I beg your pardon,
I will not share your load.

Parting is sweet sorrow—
Or so the ballads say…
But that is for tomorrow,
When you go on your way.

I'll share with you my finest wine
And mushrooms from the glen
The last time that we two shall dine
Till you come back again.

I hope it brings you pleasure—
Whatever 'tis you lack…
But for me, the greatest treasure
Will be seeing you come back.

So raise a glass in parting,
but grant me just one boon—
Although your trip's just starting,
Say it will be ending soon.

Ain't That The Way?

Mary Jane lived a "remainder" life—
she wore hand-me-down clothes.
She was a second-hand wife....

Thomas wanted a country-club home,
with two point five offspring,
and a license to roam.

Peter, he felt he had paid his dues.
He had put in his time—
he had nothing to lose....

Mary pretended—long as she could—
that her marriage was fine...
that her home-life was good.

They met one night through a quirk of fate.
She got lost in the rain—
Peter's meeting ran late.

Under the glow of a neon moon
they whispered like school-kids....
It was over too soon.

Drifting together from need, not lust...
they clung in the silence—
slowly learning to trust.

Secretive phone-calls and fleeting trysts….
They met in the shadows.
Meanwhile, Thomas got pissed.

It ended badly—as these things can
with blood in an alley
like a crimson fan.

The Soul Of A Harper

Oh, they say 'tis a hanging
that soon I will be—
My body a-twisting from
yonder oak tree—
For daring to think that a man
could live free...
but though I may die,
'tis a harper I'll be.

The strings of my harp
will never be stilled
while the green of the shamrock
still grows on the hill
for the music of Ireland
is her strength and her will
and the soul of a harper
no mortal can kill.

Oh, the red-headed queen on her
cold golden throne
fears harper freedom
she never has known
Our bright Gaelic passion
comes through in the tone
so she orders it silenced
and broods all alone.

For a man of the road,
death holds no sting.
'Tis another adventure—
a wondrous thing.
And I know that my music
will evermore ring
in the hills and the rivers
of each Irish spring.

Midnight Encounter

Clutching a lily,
she stands in the shimmering
nimbus of a street lamp—
the feathery edge of
an ermine collar brushing
a face pale as the snow
beneath her feet.

Hair of silken jet
lifts gently in
an unfelt wind
and eyes of midnight
burn with the depth
of centuries.

She waits, with breath
held unconsciously
for hours,
needing no succor
from the frosted air.

He comes along the empty street—
rushing home to a wife or lover,
soon to be forgotten in the
darkness of her eyes.

A stutter of sound to
draw his attention;
a throaty laugh when it is done.
A kiss to sweeten
chill breath on a pulsing throat.

The sleet falls red.

The Standing Stones

Ancient guardians
of time and secrets,
the stone giants
lean and whisper
of their youth.

Fair Celtic maidens
and handsome swain
cavorted in their shadows
singing in the dawn.

The whisperers remember
when the age was new,
and shadows had not fallen
across the broad moor.

The Standing Stones
keep well their secrets
teasing with memories
that only the dead
can know.

Ride The Red Wind

Brimstone and ash
rain down from a
blood red sky.
Coal black ravens
wheel the crimson clouds
with haunting cry.
Death rides a skeletal mare,
scythe glinting in the
scarlet light.
And the red wind
blows a mournful tune,
heralding endless night.
It's a witch wind blowing
amid the stars so bright,
howling a madman's song
and the only way through
the maze tonight
is to follow right along...

The Bridge Of Birds

Tonight, I am climbing the bridge of birds,
to meet my love for one night of joy.
The wrath of Heaven is a cumbersome thing…

My lot in life is to weave the clouds.
It was once enough, but I fell to dreams.
I looked away from my loom for but an instant.

And there beneath my feet was a boy.
He was tending to his herd
on the banks of a river.

He drew me to him as a flame does
a moth…and my wings caught fire.
He bound me to the earth.

I was happy to be bound.

Life was simple as a herdsman's wife.
I cooked and cleaned and tended my children.
And the clouds grew tattered and neglected.

The Queen of Heaven glared down,
angry that I chose to fall from grace
for the sake of a mortal.

She ordered me back to Heaven,
to weave, once more, the clouds
and moonbeams.
I was torn from my family
and shackled to my loom…

He followed me to Heaven,
my herdboy—
wearing the hide of his favorite ox.

The Queen of Heaven is a jealous goddess.
She denied my love despite his pain.
Scratching a river between us,
a chasm of stars too wide to ford.

I sit at my loom—
He sits on the shore—
The children call to me,
but I cannot answer back.

My heart cries out,
and my tears fall like stars,
deepening the river
that I so long to cross.

The birds saw my plight
and their hearts swelled in pity.
They twittered compassion
and offered a way.

Tonight, I am climbing a bridge
built of birds—feathered backs
entwining in a living span—

One night of joy in a year of pain
to hold my children
and dance with my love.

The Starlight Bathing...

The starlight bathing
a lover's kiss
began its journey
a thousand years
before the limbs entwining
walked the earth.

Its white hot spark
glowed to life
long before Elizabeth reigned.
Shakespeare's lovers
spoke of other stars
in sensual sonnets.

Victoria's dark streets
were touched by other light
than this.
Ageless wisdom
speaks from the mask
of limitless space...

Starlight, star bright...
what wonders have you seen?

About The Cover Artist:

Charles Ligocky is a

contemporary, abstract artist living and working in a part of Texas, USA which closely borders Mexico. Ligocky's work is influenced by a mix of tragic events and childhood memories that represent themselves on canvas and with the sculptural form. Ligocky is very private as an artist, concerning his working process and its relationship to his life and his own personal experiences. He considers all of his ideas, his thoughts and his research and he brings them out into the open by recording these things in sketchbooks.

He is concerned with these personal themes as a starting point rather than a desperate aim to express and communicate with the viewer. An important part of his creative process is the way he selects and edits from events in his life. He says about his work, "I've isolated the most important parts of my childhood and early life to take shape in my own form… Through my own vision."

Yearly Reminders Sponsored By
The House Of The Fighting Chupacabras Press
and the *Chupacabra Nation* in general:

OCTOBER

is

NATIONAL CHUPACABRA AWARENESS MONTH

and

OCTOBER 5TH

is

BRING YOUR CHUPACABRA TO WORK OR SCHOOL DAY